Copyright © 2021 In2Pickle, LLC. All Rights Reserved

ACKNOWLEDGMENTS

This sort of project would not be possible without the support of those around us. I am thankful for my wife Jill, who is my sounding board to bounce around ideas – some good and some less than optimal but all for the love of this game. Neither of us know where this In2Pickle path will lead us but she is supportive all the same even when I roll out of bed before the rooster crows to work on a new slide concept or to edit a book section. Thank you, Jilly.

Also invaluable in creating this book was Nan, a former instructional design/educator and current pickleball addict. She pushed, pulled, and cajoled me into producing what I think turned out as one of the better roadmaps available to new players. Thank you for your tireless efforts Nan.

Lastly, even though they may not have been directly involved in the production of the book, I thank all of the pickleball community who have been a part of our growth in the game, including those players on videos who I have not yet met in person but feel like I know after hours of watching them on screen.

This book has been updated since its original publication in 2020 to incorporate the 2021 modifications to the IFP pickleball rules.

Tony Roig

Your Pickleball Home

Your Pickleball Journey

The slogan for a popular table game could have been written for pickleball:

a minute to learn …
… a lifetime to master

You can play pickleball after only a few initial instructions. You can then spend an entire lifetime working to master the game.

In this Guide, you will receive the initial instructions to get started:

- What you need to play and where you can find courts and games
- How to play and keep score
- Even some pickleball strategy to get you off on the right foot

All that you need to start playing pickleball is included in this Guide.

In addition to the Guide, we have prepared a series of videos that go along with this Guide. You can access all of the videos and other supplemental written materials at our Getting Started Series Catalog at In2Pickle.com.

You will be able to learn pickleball. Trust us and the thousands who have learned before you who are still playing. People just like you. Some with sports experience and others with none. Some young and others young at heart. Some physically impaired and others not.

Follow along in this Guide and you will know everything you need to get out there playing pickleball as soon as possible.

After you play a few times, you will be ready for some more advanced concepts and strategies. Start with the Strategies in this Guide. When you want more, visit us at In2Pickle.com. We will be here as a resource for your growth in the game.

Jill and I are confident in saying that pickleball can improve your life – physically, spiritually, and emotionally. We were lucky to be introduced to pickleball by a friend and are grateful for the opportunity to share this amazing sport with you.

Join us on the journey,

Jill & Tony

Table of Contents

What You Need to Play

Throughout the Guide we will indicate when additional information is available in the Getting Started Catalog or on our website by pointing you to the "Catalog" or "Website." Visit In2Pickle.com for more.

You need three things to play pickleball: a paddle, a ball, and court shoes (preferably one for each foot). In this section, we provide information about each to help you get the equipment that is right for you.

Remember to bring your general-use items to the court: sunscreen, cap or visor, safety goggles, sweatband, towel, water bottle, etc.

The Pickleball Paddle

For your initial paddle, we recommend buying something better than the four-pack paddle available on Amazon or big box store. Boxed sets of pickleball paddles and balls are not your best investment. Borrow or try a paddle a few times from a friend or your local recreation center. If you want to go ahead and buy a paddle, here are some recommendations:

Shape

For your first paddle, we recommend a "traditional" shaped paddle. These are examples of traditional shaped paddles.

Longer pickleball paddles are good for certain special uses, like singles, but are not recommended by us for your first paddle or for general use.

Material

We recommend any of the generally available materials with two exceptions: wood cores tend to be too heavy and Nomex cores can be too harsh on the arm.

Weight

We recommend paddles between 7 and 8 ounces (definitely under 9 ounces).

Grip

Grip size and length are important. If you have small hands, look for a grip that is 4 ¼ inches or smaller in circumference. If you use a two-handed backhand (or want to), you will want a grip length of at least 5 inches.

Price

You can find a good paddle for $40-60 and an excellent paddle for $90-100. While you can spend up to $175 for a paddle, this sort of expenditure is not necessary to get a good paddle.

Picking a Paddle

During our pickleball travels, we come across many players using paddles that, in our opinion, are not suited for their game. When we ask players how they choose their paddle, the most common answer is "because that is what someone at my club uses" or "my friend told me to get it."

Avoid picking a paddle just because others are using it. Try it out first and make sure it is right for you. Another option to help you narrow your choices is to take our short "test" to see what paddles are recommended based on your personal profile:

- Have you played other racket sports?
- Are you comfortable holding weight in your hand for more than a few minutes?
- Do you need a small or longer grip?

- Do you have a paddle budget?

You can access our Paddle Guide for New Players at the Website.

The Pickleball

There are two types of balls generally used: indoor and outdoor. There is also what we term a "hybrid" ball that provides an interesting option, particularly if you are just getting into the game.

When distinguishing "outdoor" from "indoor" play for shoes and balls, we are referring to the surface of play and not the fact of being inside or outside. Indoors refers to wood or polished concrete floors like in gyms. Outdoor refers to a tennis court surface, usually rough, regardless of whether the tennis court is under a roof.

Outdoor balls will generally not play well on gym floors because they are designed for the rough surface of tennis courts. Indoor balls are the opposite: good on gym floors but not designed for rougher surfaces. Hybrid balls will work on either surface.

Hybrid Balls

If you are a beginner, start with one of the hybrid balls pictured above. The hybrid balls offer the best "feel" for someone getting started in the game, will generally not break, and will provide you with countless hours of enjoyable game play. Regardless of these balls being labeled as "outdoor" balls, you can also use them indoors or out.

Onix Pure 2

Penn 40

VIPickleball

Indoor Balls

Indoor balls are the softest of the balls and will last longer than outdoor balls. Indoor balls usually do not break – they just get too soft for continued use.

Indoor balls are often provided by the facility where you will be playing. If you want to buy indoor balls, just get a 3- or 6-pack (the above options are good choices). The Jugs ball is one of the original balls used for indoor pickleball. The Onix Fuse ball is slightly harder and will give you play that is more similar to an outdoor ball (still can be used indoors though).

Onix Fuse

The Jugs

Outdoor Balls

For outdoor play, you will usually need to have your own ball with you. Outdoor balls are made of a harder plastic and will break after some play. You will usually want to buy 6 or 12 (if not more) at a time.

The Dura Fast 40 and Franklin X-40 are the most commonly used outdoor balls. Both of these balls are made of harder plastic than the hybrid balls, will not bounce as high, and will normally crack at some point. We recommend transitioning to these balls once you are ready for them or if you are playing in a tournament.

Dura Fast 40

Franklin X-40

VIPickleball

Pickleball Shoes

If you come from racquet sports, you likely already know the difference between athletic shoes suitable for court sports and shoes that might cause injury. Otherwise, read on.

Unless your doctor has specifically told you otherwise, **DO NOT** play pickleball in jogging or other non-court shoes. The design of those shoes lacks lateral stability required when you play a sport like pickleball. If you wear improper shoes, you can:

- more easily roll or break your ankle
- cause long-term damage to the ligaments in your knee
- catch the edge of the wide heel, fall, and hurt yourself

Tennis and pickleball shoes are designed with flatter soles and wider toes for lateral movement. Jogging shoes are designed for forward movement but not for side-to-side movement. Pickleball involves a lot of lateral movement and having the right type of shoe is key to avoiding injury.

If you are playing outdoors, wear tennis or pickleball shoes that are designed for this use. If you are playing mostly indoors, you can wear volleyball or badminton shoes – these shoes will generally wear out too fast in outdoor play. If you are playing both indoors and outdoors, you can use an outdoor shoe for both.

Improper Shoes

Walking shoe

Jogging shoe

Casual wear shoe

Proper Shoes

Women's
tennis shoe

Men's
Tyrol shoe

Men's
tennis shoe

Women's Tyrol
shoe

That is all the equipment you need to play pickleball. There are other things that you should have – water, sunscreen, and maybe a visor or cap and safety eyewear – but shoes, paddle, and balls are a necessity for play. Visit the Website for our complete checklist of pickleball gear.

Let's lace up our shoes, grab our paddle, and get ready to play!

VIPickleball

Where to Play

You have your paddle, balls, shoes, and a few friends. You are ready to play. Where though?

In this section, you will learn about different options for where to play pickleball. You will discover how to find courts and play in your area. Even if there are no pickleball facilities in your area, you will be able to get started in this lifetime sport.

Dedicated Courts

If you are fortunate, there are permanent, dedicated pickleball courts near you. These courts have permanent nets and are dedicated only to pickleball. Unless the courts are clearly open to the public, ask if the courts are members-only or open to the public. Then ask if there are "open play" times.

"Open play" times are when players show up to the courts for play without having a set or private group. There is generally a system for players to rotate on and off the courts. Open play can be skill-level specific or open to anyone.

Below is a picture of a dedicated pickleball court at a county park. The court in the picture is open to the public. Open play at these courts is arranged by local players. This picture shows the customary paddle tap at the net at the end of a game.

Pre-lined Tennis or Basketball Courts

Another common option is to play on existing tennis or basketball courts with painted pickleball boundary lines. You play on these courts using temporary removable nets, often available for your use at the facility. Some painted-line courts use the existing tennis net. A tennis net is slightly higher than a pickleball net. If you are using the tennis net, you have two options:

1. If there is a middle strap on the net, slide it over an inch or so to lower the net (remember to return the strap to the center after play).
2. Leave the net as it is – you can still enjoy a great game of pickleball with a regular tennis net.

This type of court may not be as regularly occupied with pickleball players as dedicated courts are, so make sure you check availability for open play or bring friends for a game.

This is a painted court that uses one side of a tennis court (two pickleball courts can fit the length of a tennis court). The net is a temporary removable net.

The Non-Volley Zone (also known as the NVZ or "Kitchen") lines are the lines where the players are standing.

The white lines behind their feet are tennis court lines. Other than potential for distraction, these lines do not affect pickleball play.

This is a painted pickleball court that is centered within the tennis court. In this setup, the same net is used for pickleball and tennis.

You can see from this picture that the pickleball court is barely longer than the serve boxes on the tennis court (one foot on each side to be exact).

Indoor Courts

You can often find indoor pickleball courts at community recreation centers, churches, schools, YMCAs, and indoor tennis centers. Indoor courts are generally wood (gym floor/ basketball court), textured hard court (tennis), or smooth concrete (hockey arena).

These courts usually offer pickleball open play on a set schedule. Contact your local facilities to find out the pickleball schedule. Also ask if they offer beginner clinics for players - a great way to start in the sport.

An indoor court with permanent indoor lines at the Nottingham University Campus athletic facility.

Notice the other lines (red and blue in color) on the gym floor are used for other sports, such as volleyball and basketball.

Indoor courts at a YMCA center in Ohio. The participants were taking a free beginners' fundamental clinic.

Tennis Courts

You can also play on a regular tennis court with no pickleball lines. You will need some markers to denote the boundaries, which only takes a couple of minutes. You can also play a form of singles by just using the service boxes on the tennis court. We provide you more flexible game playing in the Games section of this Guide.

The following picture shows how vinyl strips are used to mark off the court. The tennis service line is used as the pickleball baseline (back line). The service line is only one foot shorter than a regulation pickleball court. This difference is not enough to mark a separate baseline of the court for recreation play.

The Catalog includes our video about playing on a tennis court.

Any Flat Surface

If none of the previous options are available near you, you can still enjoy a game of pickleball on any flat surface: basketball court, driveway, parking lot, just to name a few. You will need a space approximately 60 feet (18.5 meters) long by 30 feet (9 meters) wide, to be safe. The court dimensions measure 44 feet (13.41 meters) long by 20 feet (6.10 meters) wide.

You can mark off the court with stripes, chalk, or any other sort of marks – just make sure they are safe so no one trips over them. You can use a temporary pickleball net, a badminton net, or just some rope with paper or stringers hanging from it.

You can download court dimensions from the Catalog.

The picture on the left shows players enjoying a game on tiles in front of an apartment building in India. The right picture shows a court marked off with the same strips used on the tennis court above. Both use a temporary removable net.

Finding Places to Play

The following include helpful tips to help you find places to play:

- A good place to start is by searching places2play.org. Be specific in your search by entering a city, township, or zip code. If you use a general area search on the site, you may miss available nearby locations unless you also look using the interactive map provided.
- Call your local YMCA or community recreation centers. They are good resources and often have pickleball on their website.
- There are many Facebook pickleball groups – see if there is one for your area or for any area you may be visiting.

When you find a place, reach out to the contact person listed to confirm play dates and times. Remember that the person listed is a volunteer. He or she is usually a good resource to point you in the right direction.

You will find that most pickleball players are welcoming and willing to lend a hand to help others experience this amazing lifetime sport.

How to Hit the Pickleball

Even if you are comfortable with racket or paddle sports (tennis, table tennis, racquetball), some of the stroke concepts in this section can help you become a better pickleball player.

You are ready to play but unsure how to hit the pickleball. In this section, you will learn the basics for how to hit a groundstroke and a volley – the two shots you need to play pickleball. If you have never picked up a paddle or racket before, have no fear. Pickleball shots are easy to learn.

We will explain the basic mechanics of each shot, then display some pictures to help you visualize the proper stroke mechanics. There are several stroke videos to help you along in the Catalog. By the end of this lesson, you should be able to:

- Hold your pickleball paddle comfortably
- Hit a pickleball serve, return, and other groundstrokes
- Hit a pickleball volley
- Most importantly, be ready to go out there and play pickleball

How to Hold (Grip) Your Paddle

Before you can hit the ball, you need to know how to hold a paddle (we call it "grip" the paddle). If you already have a paddle, go grab it to follow along. If your paddle is not handy, read on but also come back to this section later with your paddle. Having a good paddle grip foundation will be more comfortable and will allow you to play better pickleball.

The best grip to use when playing pickleball is called the continental grip – sometimes referred to as the "handshake" grip. You are literally shaking hands with your paddle.

You will use the same grip for your forehand and backhand shots – we will cover more on forehand and backhand shots below.

You will know you are using the continental grip when you hold your paddle out in front of you, without twisting your arm:

- the "V" of your hand is in line with the edge of the paddle and
- the paddle face is 90 degrees to the court.

This is the continental grip   This is not the continental grip

TRY IT NOW!

1. Align your hand with the paddle as shown on the above charts. If it helps, you can place the "V" of your hand on the paddle edge and slide it down to the handle.
2. Put your arm at your side, relax it, and bring the paddle forward
3. Is the paddle 90 degrees to the floor?
   - **YES:** Great – you have a continental grip
   - **NO:** try to align your hand again (Visit the Catalog for helpful videos)

The illustrations on the next page may help you hold your paddle with the continental grip (you can download full-size versions of the charts in the Catalog).

> You will come across players not using the continental grip. While there is nothing wrong with other grips, it is best to use the continental grip if you can. It is the most versatile grip and gives you the ability to improve as you learn the game.

Grip Chart for Left-Handed Player

This is the target grip:	Continental Grip	Purple on 1 and Orange on 8
These two grips are the most common "trouble" grips:	Western Grip	Purple on 4 and Orange on 5
	Semi Western Grip	Purple on 7 and Orange on 6

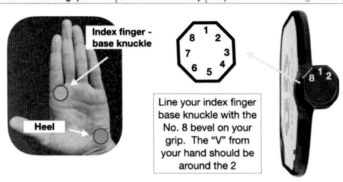

Index finger - base knuckle

Heel

Line your index finger base knuckle with the No. 8 bevel on your grip. The "V" from your hand should be around the 2

Grip Chart for Right-Handed Player

This is the target grip:	Continental Grip	Purple on 1 and Orange on 2
These two grips are the most common "trouble" grips:	Western Grip	Purple on 4 and Orange on 5
	Semi Western Grip	Purple on 3 and Orange on 4

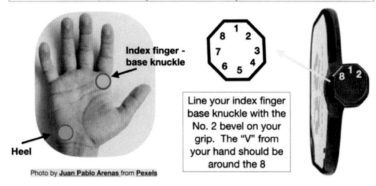

Index finger - base knuckle

Heel

Line your index finger base knuckle with the No. 2 bevel on your grip. The "V" from your hand should be around the 8

Photo by **Juan Pablo Arenas** from **Pexels**

VIPickleball

Grip Pressure

Now that you know the continental paddle grip, understanding grip pressure and paddle sides will help you as we move into specific shot mechanics.

Pickleball is best played with a medium to light grip pressure on your paddle grip. A tight hold on the grip will not help you hit better and may actually hurt your arm. Use a medium grip pressure when you first start playing – we will show you how below. You will learn more about changing grip pressures as you work to improve your game.

TRY IT NOW!

1. Hold your paddle – is it a continental grip?
2. Squeeze the grip as hard as you can.
3. Now release half the pressure from the grip.
4. That is it – that is the grip pressure you want to use when you are starting to play.

Paddle Sides

You can hit a shot from a forehand or a backhand side. The forehand side is the side of the paddle that would hit the ball when you swing the paddle on your dominant side. The backhand side is the other side of the paddle.

As you study the pictures in this section and watch videos about how to hit the ball, keep in mind the difference between a forehand and a backhand. If you are hitting on your dominant side, your shot should be a forehand. If you are hitting across your body (on the side opposite your dominant hand), your shot should be a backhand. Using both sides of your paddle is best to improve your game.

Forehand Side

Backhand Side

How to Hit a Groundstroke

Now that you can grip the paddle, you are ready to learn your first shot: the groundstroke.

> The groundstroke is one shot that is used for many purposes: serve, return of serve, dink, and any time that the ball bounces on the court ("ground") before being hit ("stroke").

Ready to serve

Forehand return of serve

One-handed backhand groundstroke

Two-handed backhand groundstroke

Forehand dink (short groundstroke)

Backhand dink

In this section, you will learn the "pendulum" swing groundstroke. The pendulum swing is the stroke foundation endorsed by the International Pickleball Teaching Professional Association (IPTPA). The pendulum swing originates from your shoulder, relies on the natural motion of your arm, and will provide you with a fundamentally-sound stroke for years of pickleball play.

How the Pendulum Swing Works

To use the pendulum swing, you will be swinging almost entirely from your shoulder – just like a pendulum. Your groundstrokes will be hit along the arc (or curve) created by swinging your paddle as a pendulum.

Your arm should remain straight during the swing. Not stiff, but relaxed and straight. If you lay a broomstick from your shoulder to your paddle, your shoulder, arm and paddle face should remain in line with the broomstick. If you bend your elbow or wrist, you will no longer be in line with the broomstick.

Straight arm – but relaxed   Bent wrist – breaking the straight arm

Swinging from the shoulder makes for less variation in your paddle angle. Less variation in your paddle angle will make for a more consistent game.

You will swing the paddle from the shoulder. Elbow and wrist movement should be minimal during the swing. These images are of the forehand pendulum swing. There are step-by-step instructions for how to swing the paddle below. You can also follow along with the videos in this series.

The backhand pendulum swing is similar to the forehand pendulum swing. Your paddle will not travel as far back, and you will be using the "back" side of the paddle. Otherwise, it is the same as the forehand pendulum swing: relaxed straight arm swinging from the shoulder.

The pendulum swing is the foundation for your groundstrokes. Get comfortable with it before moving on to the next sections. Once you are feeling comfortable with the swing, try it with your eyes closed.

You want to be able to do the swing without thinking about it. Practicing this technique will train your muscle memory for every shot. The same way your legs use muscle memory when you walk (you do it every day without thinking HOW you do it), you also want to swing your paddle without thinking about it.

1. Stand with the paddle at your side. Use the continental grip with medium grip pressure. Bend your knees a little – this will get you into the ready position.

2. Start with the forehand side. Swing the paddle on your left side if you are lefthanded and right side if you are righthanded. The paddle should swing naturally along the arc/curve of the pendulum created from your shoulder.

3. Keep your arm relaxed but straight – minimize bending at elbow or wrist. Notice that the paddle is naturally "open" at about 45 degrees when the paddle is reached forward with a straight arm.

4. Keep swinging a few times, making sure the paddle is swinging from the shoulder. It may help if you do this in front of a mirror so you can see the swing.

5. Switch to the backhand side and try it a few times. Swing along the arc from the shoulder keeping a straight relaxed arm.

You can follow along with the How to Hit videos in the Catalog.

How to Hit Groundstrokes

Now that you understand the pendulum swing, let's put it together in the groundstroke.

It is useful to group groundstrokes into two categories – long and short:

- Long groundstroke – serve and return – travel farther.
- Short groundstrokes – dinks – travel a shorter distance.

Generally, you will use a stronger grip pressure for long groundstrokes and a lighter grip pressure as the groundstrokes become shorter. Focus on grip pressures after you have learned the other basics in this Guide. For now, use a medium grip pressure.

Also, generally, your swing will be longer when you hit long groundstrokes than when you hit shorter groundstrokes.

Only swing the paddle only as far as necessary for the shot – not more. You will learn more about backswing (before you hit the ball) and follow through (after you hit the ball) as you grow in the sport.

Long Groundstroke

For long groundstrokes, bring your paddle down slightly more along the arc (not behind the plane of your body) and finish higher along the arc.

Short Groundstroke

For short groundstrokes, bring your paddle down along the same arc, but shorten the swing.

VIPickleball

Try the forehand first (steps 1-4). Then the backhand.

1. Start with the natural arc of the pendulum using your paddle.

2. Stop the paddle at the top of the arc – not too high. If you like to think in terms of angles, think 45 degrees. This will be the end of your stroke.

3. From the top of the arc, pull the paddle backwards to near your leg. This is as far back as you will want to bring the paddle, even for the longest groundstrokes.

4. Practice a few swings between these two points – the starting point near your leg and the ending point at approximately a 45-degree angle. This is the groundstroke.

> The actual length of your swing will depend on how long or short you are hitting the ball, but these starting and ending points provide a good visual regarding swing length.

You can follow along with the How to Hit videos in the Catalog.

How to Serve

> The pickleball serve is the first shot during a rally.

The pickleball serve is a long groundstroke. There are two ways you can hit your serve: (1) from the air before the ball bounces –the "traditional" or "in-air" serve or (2) after the ball has bounced – this is a new serve allowed by the rules and is called the "drop serve."

If you are just getting started playing pickleball, we recommend starting with the drop serve. It is basically a groundstroke where you feed the ball to yourself. The only rule is that you must drop the ball before you serve it. You cannot push (propel) the ball downwards – it has to literally be a drop. After that, you can hit the ball however you like.

The following images illustrate the steps for a drop serve:

Drop ball from a height where it will bounce up enough for you to serve.

Ball should bounce in front of you. It can bounce inside or outside the court.

You hit the ball along the pendulum swing of the groundstroke.

Your feet must be behind the baseline when you hit the serve, as shown in the images.

VIPickleball

If you wish to try the in-air serve, you must comply with the following rules:

1. Hit the ball in the air without being bounced.
2. Contact with the ball must not be made above the waist level (Waist is defined as the navel level).
3. The highest point of the paddle head must not be above the highest part of the wrist.
4. The server's arm must be moving in an upward arc at the time the ball is struck.

As with the drop serve, your feet must be behind the baseline when you hit the serve, as shows in the below images.

The following images illustrate the steps for an in-air serve:

Swing starts at the back of the pendulum arc swing. Note that the body is turned (the paddle is not pulled behind the body).

Contact is made as the paddle travels along the pendulum arc swinging from the shoulder.

The swing ends at the front (top) of the pendulum swing.

Your feet must be behind the baseline when you hit the serve, as shown in the images.

When you use the pendulum swing to hit your serve, you will likely comply with the serve motion rules.

If you are learning how to serve a pickleball, bouncing the ball first is a good way to practice and learn. If you are playing at a recreation center or open play, you will be expected to hit the ball before it bounces. Be prepared and practice.

How to Dink

> The dink is a short groundstroke that is intended to land inside the NVZ on the other side of the net.

The pickleball "dink" is a shot that is unique to the sport of pickleball. When executed properly, the dink cannot be volleyed by the opponent rendering it unattackable. The dink has the same pendulum swing as the long groundstrokes, but with a shorter swing.

This illustration shows the NVZ, which is the area between the net and the parallel line that is 7 feet from the net (the "NVZ line"). You will get familiar with the movement on the court, including the NVZ rules in the Playing section of this Guide. For now, it is helpful to understand that the existence of the NVZ is what makes the dink shot such an important part of the game.

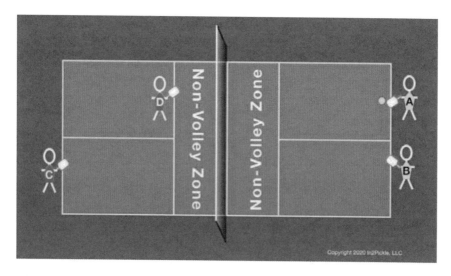

Copyright 2020 In2Pickle, LLC

These pictures show what a dink looks like "in action."

1. Short backswing before hitting the ball. Hitting ball out in front of the body. Eyes on the contact zone (where the paddle will hit the ball).

2. Short follow through and back to ready position. Ball has good clearance over the net (try not to hit the net). It might help to think about the shot as "tossing" the ball into the NVZ when you hit it.

3. Ball lands inside the opponent's NVZ so that the opponent cannot volley the ball, which makes it unattackable.

TRY IT NOW!

1. Stand at the NVZ line. Hold the ball at the bottom of the pendulum (the beginning of the swing arc). Keep the ball in front of your body. This is a forehand toss.
   If you are at home, you can do this drill tossing the ball to another person or just tossing it onto a sofa or chair.

✓IPickleball

2. Toss the ball over the net (or other props – ideally about 8-10 feet away), and get it to land inside the NVZ on the other side.

The toss should be a natural swing originating from your shoulder (the pendulum swing).

You can now try the dink with the paddle. Follow along with the above images of the dink in action. Your paddle swing should be (and feel) similar to the hand-toss motion.

Several drills and exercises, including how to dink are available at the Website.

VIPickleball

How to Hit a Volley

The volley is where the ball is hit out of the air; the ball does not bounce on the court.

After you have learned the groundstroke, you still need to learn the volley to play pickleball. The volley is when you hit the ball out of the air (no bounce on the court). The ball does not have to be above your head in order for it to be a volley. Any time you contact the ball before it bounces during a rally, you have volleyed it.

Forehand groundstroke

Forehand volley

Hinging the Wrist

Pickleball groundstrokes can be hit with a "natural" unhinged wrist but volleys will usually require a hinged wrist. Hinging your wrist will turn the paddle relative to your arm as shown below.

Unhinged forehand grip

Hinged forehand grip

Unhinged backhand grip

Hinged backhand grip

Paddle Swing

Similar to the groundstroke, your swing during the volley should be controlled and compact. Big swings are not necessary in pickleball.

Forehand volley

Big swing   Volley start   Volley finish

Backhand volley

Big swing   Volley start   Volley finish

VIPickleball

The NVZ Rule

Where you hit a volley is important. As you play pickleball, you will spend a lot of time near the "Non-Volley Zone line" (the line that is seven feet from the net).

Perhaps the most important rule of pickleball is that you cannot be inside the NVZ when you volley the ball (the "NVZ Rule"). As the name suggests, you cannot volley the ball while standing inside of it. Remember a volley is when the ball is hit in the air.

You can step into the NVZ to hit a ball that has bounced (usually a dink). This would be a groundstroke by you. It is a fault if you volley the ball while standing in the NVZ.

Congratulations! You are now ready to hit all the shots needed to play pickleball. It is time to get out on the pickleball court and practice. After finishing this section and practicing a few times, you should be able to:

- Hold your paddle comfortably: continental grip and not too tight
- Hit serves, returns, and other groundstrokes: pendulum swing, long and short
- Hit a volley: hinged wrist, compact stroke

It is now time to go out and play pickleball. You may want to bring a copy of this Guide with you to the courts. It can provide a quick reference point if you have a question. Have fun out there.

Playing a Pickleball Game

You have your pickleball paddle, balls, shoes, a pickleball court to play on, and some friends to play with but, wait a minute, how do you *play* pickleball?

In this section, you will learn:

- How to determine which team serves first
- Where to stand for serve and return
- How to start the game
- The rules for serve, return, and playing a point
- How to move between points

When you are done with this section, you will know what you need to get out on the court and play pickleball.

Rally versus Points

Before we move on, we will be using a term that may not be familiar to you: rally. A "rally" in pickleball is the series of shots that are exchanged starting with the serve and ending with a fault or dead ball (either of these end the rally).

We will use the term "point" to mean a scored point that is earned after the serve team wins a rally. We recognize that "point" and "rally" are commonly used interchangeably but for purposes of explaining the game, it will make more sense if we use the terms according to their literal definitions.

Starting Play

A doubles pickleball game involves two teams with two players on each team. Teams play on opposite sides of a net. Doubles can be played in any combination of gender. You can play singles too (one player vs. one player). You can find information about playing singles in the Catalog.

Some of this Guide applies to both doubles and singles. For example, the serve is the same. But some of what is in this Guide is doubles specific. For example, calling the server number as part of the score. The Strategy section is also doubles specific.

How to Determine Which Team Serves First

Teams choose who will serve first. Sometimes the courts you play on will have a standing "rule" – like the closest to the back fence serves first. If not, you can just pick a number or flip a coin. In our example, the team in yellow (Players A and B) will serve first.

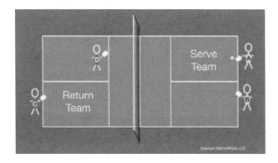

Where to Stand for Serve and Return

At the beginning of the game, the player on the right side of the court when looking at the pickleball net will always serve first. In our example, Player A is the first server.

Player B stands at the back of the court because of the Two-Bounce Rule (more on this below). Only the server is required to keep both feet behind the back line when serving.

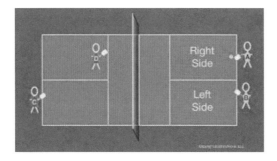

The player diagonal (cross-court) from the server – Player C – is the returner (or "receiver"). Player D will stand near the NVZ line.

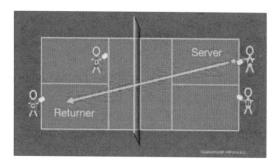

Hitting the Serve and Return

The serve must be hit into the box diagonally across from the server. This sort of shot is called "cross-court."

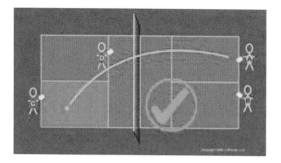

If the serve lands anywhere other than the cross-court serve box, the serve is out. If the serve is out, the serve team loses that serve.

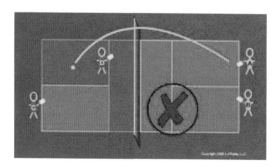

VIPickleball

Three of the lines on the serve box are part of the serve box and "in," but the line closest to the net (the NVZ line) is out on a serve. If the served ball lands on the NVZ line, the serve is out.

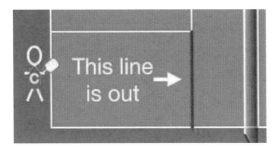

The returner must allow the ball to bounce before hitting it. The ball bouncing on this side of the court is the *first* bounce of the Two-Bounce Rule.

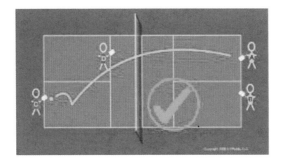

The served ball cannot be volleyed by the returner (hit in the air) until it bounces on the court. This is a fault ending the rally.

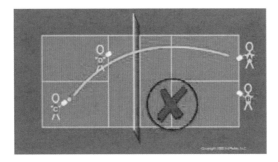

VIPickleball

The returner can hit the ball anywhere inside the serve team's side of the court. Lines are in.

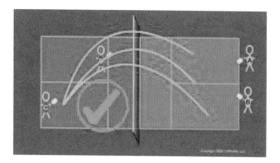

The serve team cannot hit the returned ball in the air (a volley). This is a violation of the Two-Bounce Rule and a fault ending the rally.

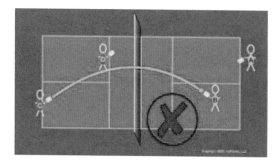

The serve team must let the returned ball bounce before hitting it. The ball bouncing on this side of the court is the *second* bounce of the Two-Bounce Rule and completes the rule for this rally.

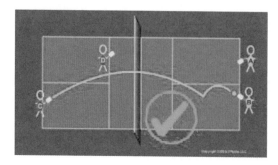

VIPickleball
Wearepickleball.com

The importance of the Two-Bounce Rule is that it allows the return team to move up to the NVZ (more on the NVZ later) before the serve team can move up.

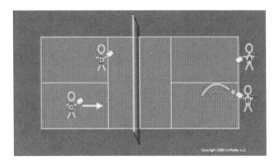

Playing the Rally/Point

After the serve and return, there are a few other rules that you will need to follow.

The NVZ
The line next to Player D (closest to the net) is called the NVZ line and the area in front of it is called the NVZ.

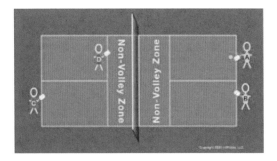

When you play pickleball, you will stand somewhere outside the NVZ. The best strategic position to play from is with your feet near the NVZ line. That is why one of the players on the return team (Player D in the above illustration) stands there at the beginning of each rally before the serve is hit. You can read more about playing up at the NVZ in the Strategy section of this Guide.

VIPickleball

The importance of the NVZ is that, as the name suggests, you cannot volley the ball while standing inside of it. The NVZ line is considered part of the NVZ. Standing on the NVZ line is the same as standing inside the NVZ.

You can step into the NVZ to hit a ball that has bounced (usually a dink). The rule includes a few other details but when you are getting started, just remember that you can enter the NVZ when the ball bounces but it is a fault if you volley the ball while standing in there.

Player C correctly hits the ball after a bounce while standing inside the NVZ.

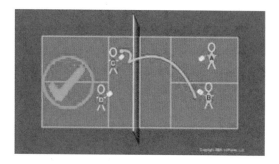

Player D commits a fault by volleying the ball while standing inside the NVZ.

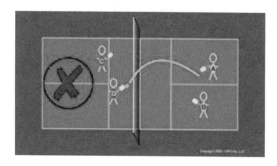

Out Balls

A ball is "in" if it lands anywhere on the other side of the net inside the lines. The lines are considered part of the "in" court. A ball that lands on the line is considered "in."

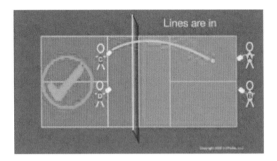

A ball that is not contacted by the opposing team and lands outside the court is "out." The rally ends on an out ball.

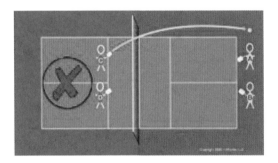

If you are unsure about whether a ball landed in or out, then the ball is "in."

✔️Pickleball

Finishing the Point

A point is played until the first of the following:

- The ball lands in the net,
- The ball lands "out",
- The ball bounces twice on the court (except in Para Pickleball where two bounces are allowed before the ball is dead on the third bounce),
- A player volleys inside the NVZ, or
- Another fault or dead ball event occurs (do not worry about these at first – they are uncommon occurrences like the ball coming into contact with the net post).

Moving Between Points/Rallies

Now that you know where to stand and what the rules are to start and play a point, let's go over some points so you can see how the players move depending on which team wins the rally. Remember that a "rally" is an exchange of shots and a "point" is a score.

Let's start a game and focus on how the players move between rallies. You will learn how to keep score in the Scoring section of this Guide.

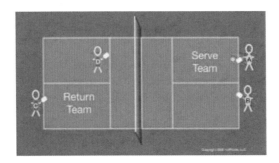

Server 1 and Server 2

Except for the first serve of the game, each time a team gets to serve (called a "side out"), both players on the team will get a chance to serve. The first server is referred to as "server 1" and the second server as "server 2." We will get into the numbers more in the Scoring section but for now what is important is to understand that, except for the first serving turn of the game, both players on each team get a chance to serve.

After each side out, the serve switches from one team to the other. The service turn for each team begins with the player who is standing on the right side of the court at the time of the side out. That player will be server 1. It may or may not be the same player between service turns.

The exception, which we mentioned above, is the team that starts serving the game will only have one player serve during the initial service turn. The player standing on the right side of the court at the beginning of the game – Player A in our example – will be the first server for the game.

VIPickleball

Scoring a Point

The yellow serving team in our example wins the first rally – earning a point. As a result, Player A switches positions with Player B and serves again. When the serve team wins, it continues serving until the return team sides them out (more below).

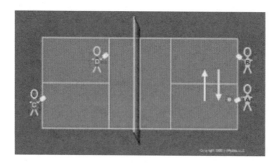

In theory, the first server can serve 11 times in a row to finish the game as long as the serve team keeps on winning (this is informally known as a "golden pickle").

Because the serve from Player A will now be from the left side, Player D will return the next serve. As a result, Player D moves back and Player C moves forward.

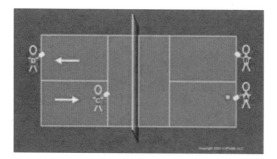

Player A serves cross-court to Player D. Player B stands at the back of the court on the right side and Player C stands at the NVZ line.

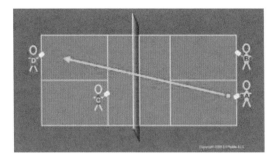

Side Out

The blue team wins the rally. Because the yellow team has no more serves left in this service turn, the serve switches from the yellow team to the blue team. This is called a "side out."

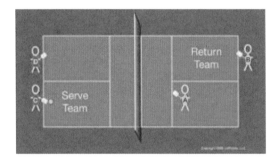

Because the blue team is now serving, Players C and D move back and Player A moves up to the NVZ line. Player C is on the right side and is server "1." Player C will serve cross-court towards Player B.

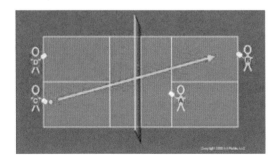

Pickleball

Second Server

The yellow team wins the rally. As a result, the blue team loses the first serve. Because each player on the blue team gets to serve during its turn, Player D will serve as server "2." Player D will serve to Player A.

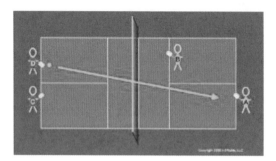

When the return team wins a rally, the players do not switch positions left to right. The only time a player switches position left to right is: (a) when the player is on the serve team and (b) the serve team wins the rally – scoring a point.

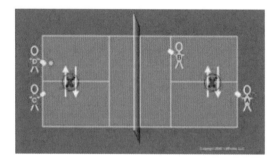

Moving Left to Right

Blue team wins the next rally, scoring a point. Player D switches places with Player C – left to right. Only the serve team moves left to right. The return team does not move left to right - only front to back.

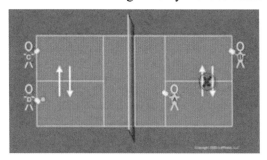

Player B moves back to return serve. Player A stands at the NVZ line.

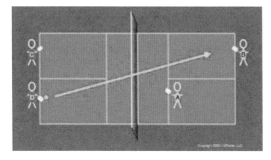

Another Side Out

Yellow team wins the next rally. Another side out. Serve switches to the yellow team. Player B, on the right at the side out, is server, "1." As usual, the serve goes cross-court to the blue team's receiving player – Player D.

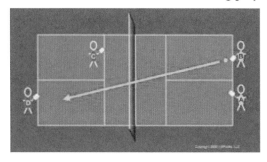

VIPickleball

Your Turn

Apply the information you learned in this section to determine what must have happened during the prior rally. Each rally immediately follows the last. Answers are on the next page. Take the time to figure these out – you will be glad you did.

1. This is where the players were standing at the beginning of the last rally before these questions. Use this image as your starting point.

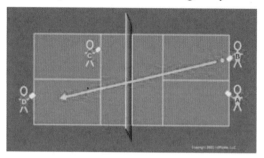

2. What happened during the previous rally (the rally that started in the image in 1, above)?

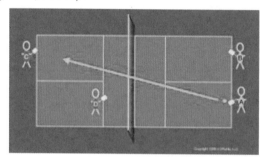

3. What happened during the previous rally (the rally that started in the image in 2, above)?

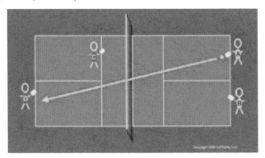

4. What happened during the previous rally (the rally that started in the image in 3, above)?

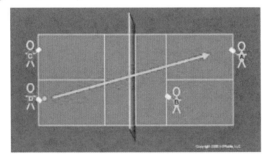

Answers

1. This is where the players were standing at the beginning of the last rally before the questions. This is our starting point.

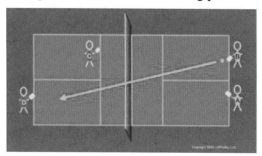

2. Blue team won the rally. We know this because Player B served the previous rally. Player B was server "1." The only way Player A can be serving on the very next rally is if the yellow team lost the first serve. Player A is the server "2."

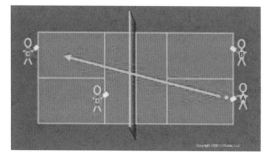

3. Yellow team won the rally. We know this because Player A served the previous rally. The only way Player A can serve again on the very next rally is if the yellow team won. Player A served from the left side last time and has now moved to the right side to serve again. Player A is server "2."

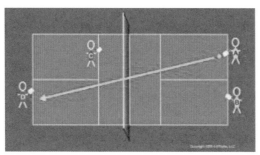

4. Blue team won the rally. We know this because Player D is now serving. The result of the last rally must have been a side out. Player D is server "1" on this service turn.

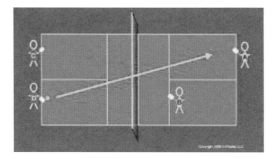

VIPickleball

Extra Credit

This is where the players were standing at the beginning of the last rally before the questions. This is our starting point.

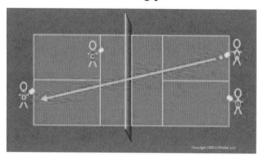

How can this be the position to start the next rally?

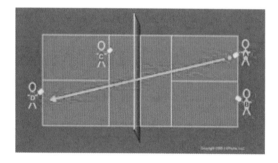

A fault by the yellow team. The only way Player A can serve again is if the yellow team won the previous rally. But the serve would have to be from the left side (switching from right to left). If Player A served a second time from the same side after winning the rally, that is a fault.

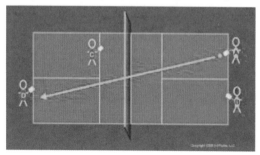

Let's review. You should now be able to:

- Determine which team serves first
- Stand in the proper location for serve and return
- Start the game
- Understand the rules for serve, return, and playing a point
- Move correctly between points

You can find a lot more tips and techniques for all levels at our In2Pickle.com website.

Scoring a Pickleball Game

Almost there. All you need to know now is how to score the game. Pickleball has a quirky scoring system that may take you a few games on the court to figure out.

By the end of this section, you will be able to:

- Keep the proper score
- Move properly between points
- Identify the first and second server on your team

To help you practice, we will use illustrations to go through an actual game, giving you the score after each rally and explaining how the game is scored. After our explanations, you will get a turn to figure out the score based on where the players are to start the next point. You will be glad you took the time now to learn scoring before you get out on the courts.

Game Start

The score at the beginning of any game is zero-zero-two (0-0-2). The score is called out as follows:

1. Serve team's score is called first,
2. Return team's score is called second,
3. Number of server is called last.

A score of 0-0-2 means that the serve team has 0 points, the return team has 0 points and the server is the second "2" server. Remember that for the first serve of the game, the serve team only gets one serve. The yellow team below is serving first and Player A is the first server of the game.

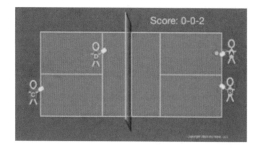

Scoring the Game

Let's score a few points and then you can test yourself.

Point Scored

Game start score:
- Serve team (yellow) – 0 points
- Return team (blue) – 0 points
- Server – 2 (game start server is the second server)

Player A calls the score 0-0-2

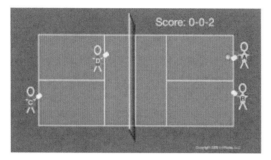

The yellow team wins the first rally (again, the "rally" is the exchange of shots beginning with the serve by Player A and ending with, for example, the blue team hitting the ball out of the court). As a result, the yellow team is awarded 1 point:
- Serve team (yellow) – 1 point
- Return team (blue) – 0 points
- Server – 2 (Player A remains second server)

Player A calls the score 1-0-2

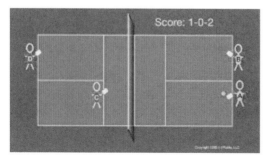

Side Out

The blue team wins the next rally. This is a side out and the serve changes to the blue team.

Because the blue team was the return team during the last rally, **it was awarded no point**. In pickleball, a point is awarded when the team wins the rally **AND** is the serve team.

- Serve team (blue) – 0 points
- Return team (yellow) – 1 point
- Server – 1 (Player C is the first server on this side out)

Player C calls the score 0-1-1

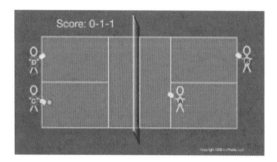

Second Server

Yellow team wins the next rally. No point is awarded – yellow team was the return team. Player D of the blue team will be the second server.

- Serve team (blue) – 0 points
- Return team (yellow) – 1 point
- Server – 2

Player D calls the score: 0-1-2

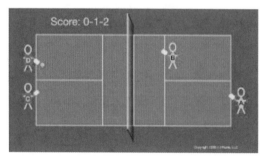

Tied Score

Blue team wins the next rally.

Because the blue team was the serve team **AND** won the rally, 1 point is awarded. The score is now tied at 1-1. Player D – the "2" server – will serve again.

- Serve team (blue) – 1 point
- Return team (yellow) – 1 point
- Server – 2

Player D calls the score: 1-1-2

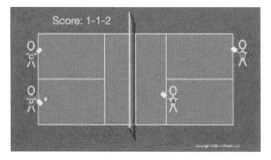

Side Out

Yellow team wins the next rally. Side out. Serve switches from blue team to yellow team. Player B is the first server for the yellow team.

The server in the score resets to "1." **The serve call (the third number) will always be either 1 or 2 – never another number.**

- Serve team (yellow) – 1 point
- Return team (blue) – 1 point
- Server – 1 (resets to 1)

Player B calls the score: 1-1-1

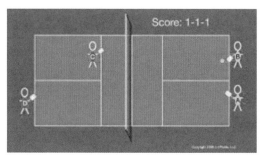

Second Server

Blue team wins the next rally. Score remains the same but the server changes from 1 to 2. Player A is the second server during this side out.

- Serve team (yellow) – 1 point
- Return team (blue) – 1 point
- Server – 2

Player A calls the score: 1-1-2

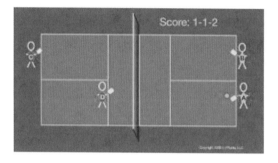

Point Scored

Yellow team wins the next rally.

- Serve team (yellow) – 2 points
- Return team (blue) – 1 point
- Server – 2 (no change)

Player A calls the score: 2-1-2

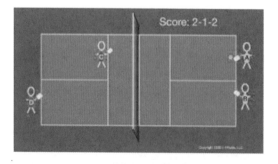

You may sometimes hear "zero-zero-start" called out at the beginning of a game. That is another way of a player calling "zero-zero-two" at the beginning of the game.

Your Turn

Test yourself by figuring out the score based on the player's court positions. These illustrations are a continuation of the above game. Each situation follows the rally directly behind it; we are just continuing the game. Take your time to work through each situation. You will feel more comfortable out on the courts if you are able to correctly call out the score.

This is how we left the game above. The rallies below will start from here.

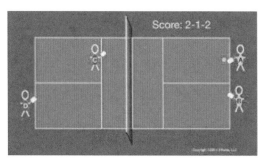

Situation 1

This is the very next rally. Player D is serving.

- What happened during the last rally?
- What is the score now?
- What server number is Player D?

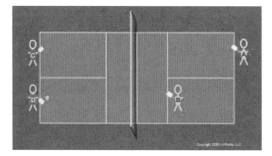

Situation 2

This is the very next rally. Player C is serving.

- What happened during the last rally?
- What is the score now?
- What server number is Player C?

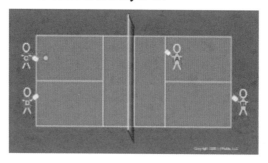

Situation 3

This is the very next rally. Player C is serving again.

- What happened during the last rally?
- What is the score now?
- What server number is Player C?

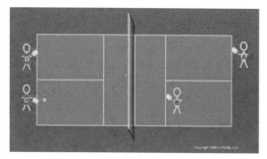

VIPickleball

Situation 4

This is the very next rally. Player A is serving.

- What happened during the last rally?
- What is the score now?
- What server number is Player A?

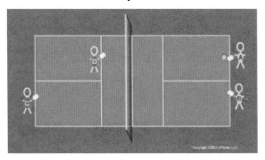

Answers

This is how we left the game above. The rallies below will start from here.

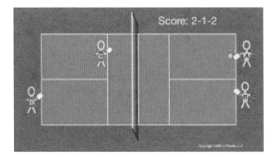

Situation 1: Answer

- Side out. Yellow team served the prior rally (see image above). For Player D to be serving now, the blue team must have won the last rally.
- Score does not change but is called in reverse order – blue team has 1 point and yellow team has 2 points.
- Player D is server 1.

Player D calls the score: 1-2-1

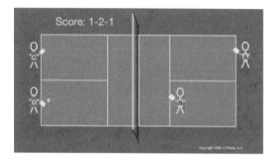

Situation 2: Answer

- Yellow team won the rally. Player D was the first serve on this side out (see prior image). The blue team lost the first serve. That is why Player C is now the server.
- Score remains the same.
- Player C is server 2.

Player C calls the score: 1-2-2

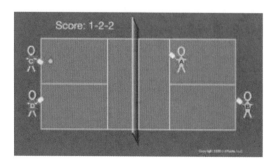

Situation 3: Answer

- Blue team won the rally. Player C has moved right to serve again.
- Because blue team won the rally **AND** was the serve team, it earned 1 point for a total of 2 points. Yellow team's score remains at 2.
- Player C remains server 2.

Player C calls the score: 2-2-2

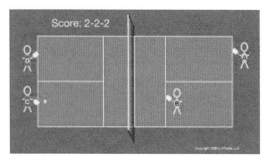

Situation 4: Answer

- Side out. Blue team served the last rally. For Player A on the yellow team to be serving now, yellow team must have won the last rally.
- Score on a side out stays the same but is called with the serve team score first and the return team score second.
- Player A is server 1.

Player A calls the score: 2-2-1

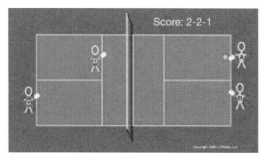

That is it - you just keep going until one team scores 11 points (or whatever score you agree on prior to play). You should now be able to keep score, move properly between points, and identify the first and second server on your team between the rallies.

Fundamental Strategy

Once you have played a few times, you will realize that there is more to pickleball than just getting the ball over the net and into the court. As mentioned at the beginning of this Guide, while you can learn pickleball in a few minutes, it can take a lifetime to master every aspect of the game. In this section, we get you started down the path by sharing some of the most important fundamentals of effective pickleball play.

The first fundamental is understanding that the strategies when you are the serve team differ from the strategies when you are the return team.

When you are the serve team, you are at a disadvantage because of the Two-Bounce Rule. The disadvantage is that your opponents (the return team) will be able to move up to the NVZ line before you. Most successful pickleball is played at the NVZ line. The following will show you how to neutralize that disadvantage and get you into position to win the rally and score a point.

When you are the return team, you have the positional advantage of being able to control the NVZ line first. The following will show you how to maintain that advantage and make it as difficult as possible for the serve team to score a point.

We will also give you some tips about playing once all players are up at the NVZ line.

Understanding these fundamental strategies will help you build a good foundation to grow in the game.

Visit the Getting Started Catalog at In2Pickle.com for all of our videos and other materials to help you understand pickleball strategy. Follow us on YouTube for the latest strategies, concepts, and skills to for your continued improvement.

The Serve Team

When you are serving, aim the ball deep, but not so deep that the serve has a high chance of going out.

Aim your serve towards the middle of the service box – 7 or 8 feet past the opponent's NVZ line. This target will provide you with room to avoid an out serve.

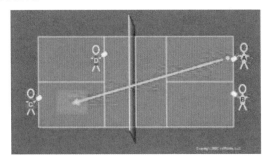

Because Players A and B have to wait for the ball to bounce (the Two-Bounce Rule), they start with a positional disadvantage compared to the blue team.

The yellow team's objective as the serve team is to neutralize the advantage of the blue team by getting up to the NVZ line.

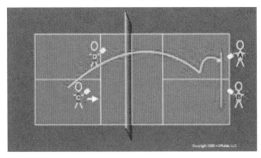

VIPickleball

As a general rule, pickleball is best played at the NVZ line. If a team can control the NVZ line and keep the other team from the NVZ line, it will win most of the rallies.

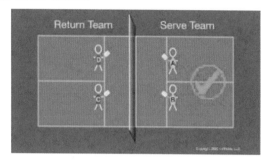

Trying to win a pickleball rally from the back of the court is very difficult and is less than optimal strategy.

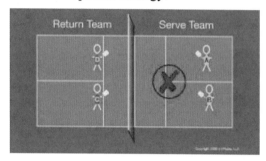

The most traditional technique for the serve team to move forward is to hit a high arcing shot called the third shot or long dink. The long dink should be hit high enough that the ball clears the top of the net but still bounces in the return team's NVZ.

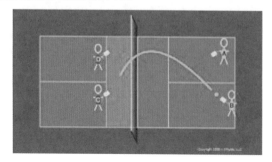

VIPickleball

This approach makes it difficult for the return team to volley/attack the ball giving the serve team more time to move forward to the NVZ line.

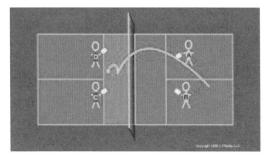

If the ball hit by the yellow team lands in or near the NVZ, the yellow serve team should move forward.

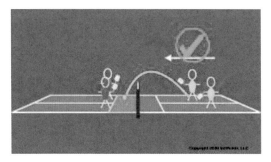

If the ball hit by the yellow team is too deep, then the blue team will probably hit it hard from a volley ("slam" it). In that case, the yellow team should stop moving forward until a better shot has been hit.

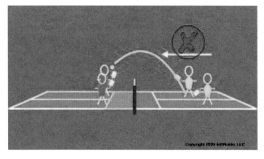

You will learn more about the third shot/long dink as you play the game. When getting started, practice a high arcing shot that clears the net and lands in your opponent's NVZ. Your objective is to get up to, and play pickleball up at, the NVZ line.

The Return Team

When you are returning the serve, hit the ball deep but not so deep that it has a high chance of going out. Remember that the serve team cannot volley the returned ball – it must bounce.

If you return it midcourt or short, though, you will give an advantage to the serve team.

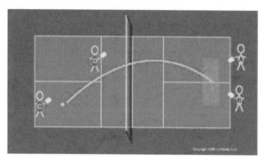

A good target for the return of serve is the center line on the court about 4-5 feet from the baseline. As soon as the return is hit, Player C should move up to the NVZ line.

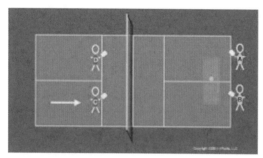

The court should look like this after the return when the yellow team is getting ready to hit the third shot.

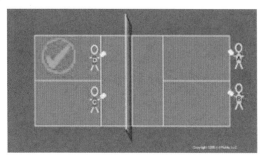

If the court looks like this, then the blue team is not taking full advantage of the Two-Bounce Rule. If Player C is here when the yellow team hits the third shot, the yellow team will have an easier time attacking Player C, moving up to the NVZ and potentially winning the rally.

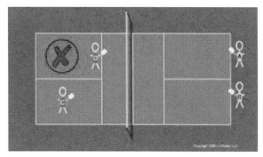

If Player C needs more time to move forward (injury, lack of speed), Player C should hit a high deep return; hit higher and deeper if more time is needed to move forward.

✓IPickleball

Once the blue team is at the NVZ line, its objective is to keep the yellow team back.

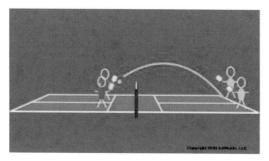

If the yellow team hits a ball that can be volleyed by the blue team and the yellow team is still back (there is space between the yellow team and the NVZ line), then the blue team should hit the ball to keep the yellow team as far back as possible. This approach keeps the yellow team at a disadvantage.

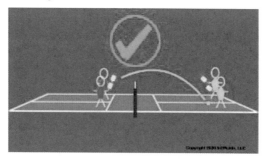

If the blue team is able to volley the ball and the yellow team has not yet made it forward to the NVZ line, the blue team should avoid hitting the ball short.

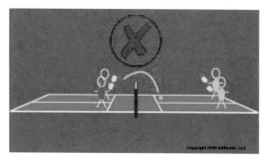

VIPickleball

A short ball invites the yellow team to move up to the NVZ line. If the yellow team makes it to the NVZ line, then the blue team's positional advantage is neutralized.

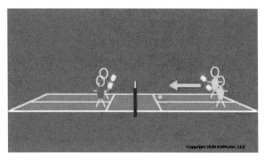

This is the back-and-forth between serve and return teams: serve team trying to move forward and the return team trying to keep them back. The team that is successful more often will likely win the game.

If the yellow team hits an effective long dink, the blue team will not be able to volley the ball. Instead, the blue team will have to let the ball bounce and will probably be hitting low to high (meaning from below the net).

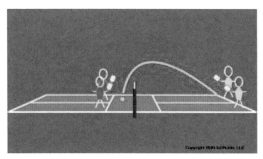

VIPickleball

Since the ball will take longer to travel and must bounce before the blue team can hit it, the yellow team will have time to move forward, maybe even making it all the way to the NVZ line before its next shot.

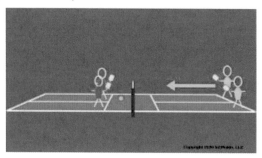

Because the blue team is more limited – it cannot volley the ball and has to hit low to high – and because the yellow team is closer to the NVZ line, the best shot here is a dink by the blue team. The dink will minimize attack by the yellow team.

A hard or deep shot from low to high from the blue team may give the yellow team an attackable shot. You should avoid giving the opponent an attackable ball.

Playing at the NVZ

Once all four players are at the NVZ line, they start a game of cat and mouse – the "soft game." When you are playing at the NVZ, try to move your opponent around with your shots. You might get a miss or a "pop up." Let's look at one example of a soft game point to give you an idea of how the point might be played.

In this point, the yellow team hit a successful long dink and made it up to the NVZ line. This is a typical scenario where all four players are at the NVZ line.

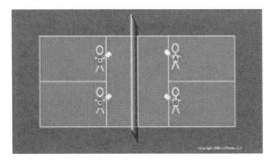

Because it was an effective long dink, Player C is forced to hit a dink back into the yellow team's NVZ – the long dink could not be volleyed and Player C was hitting low to high. Player C dinks toward Player A.

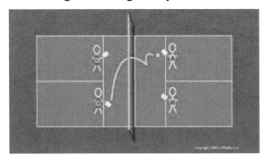

As much as possible, you want to hit your dinks so that they are unattackable by your opponent.

Player A dinks the ball back over neutrally. This means that the ball is landing in the blue team NVZ, but is not placing any stress on the blue team.

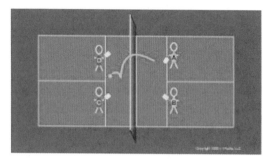

Player D dinks the ball out to the side. This dink forces Player B to move to hit the next shot. This sort of dink can "stress" the opponent and may result in an error: either a miss or a pop up.

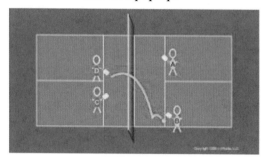

The blue team gets the intended result: Player B hits a high and deep ball that can be attacked by Player C. This is the pop up hoped for by the blue team.

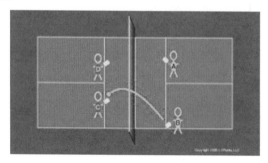

Player C can smash the popped up ball into the opening, ending the point. A pop up followed by a smash is a common way that a pickleball point ends.

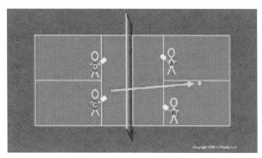

In this illustration, the ball hit by the yellow team (the dink) cannot be volleyed by the blue team. Instead, the ball will bounce in the blue team NVZ. This is a good dink.

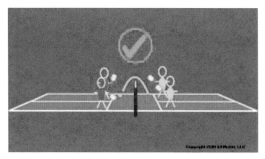

In this illustration, the ball hit by the yellow team (the attempted dink) is too deep and can be attacked / slammed by the blue team. This is a "pop up" and should be avoided.

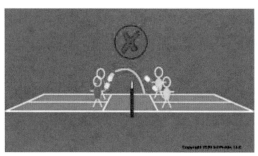

VIPickleball

Growing Your Pickleball Game

Pickleball is a strategic game – like playing chess on your feet. As you play more pickleball, you will develop strategic thinking, learn strategy from other players, and gain critical skills on situaional awareness. You will become more in tune with what is going on around you on the court. With consistent playing and practice, you will want to learn even more to advance your game. You can get more tips and strategies at the In2Pickle YouTube Channel and stay on top of your game.

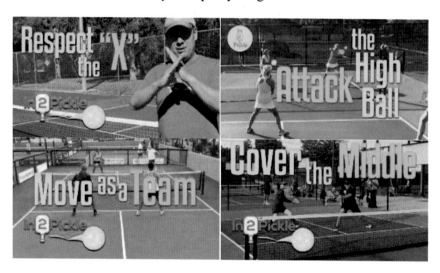

Next Step – Become a VIP

Once you are ready to really dive into, and learn, the game, join CJ Johnson and me in our immersive learning community, VIPickleball. In VIPickleball we provide you with step-by-step instruction and access to online coaching from the best instructors in the game. You can find out more about VIPickleball at wearepickleball.com.

Wearepickleball.com

Games

In this section, we share with you several modified games that you can play for practice or just for fun. Get creative with these games. These games are just some ideas to get you going. The important thing is to get out there and play.

Skinny Singles / Ghost Doubles

Those are two names for the same game. If you are going to learn just one modified game, this is it. You can play regular singles; however, playing the entire court is not for everyone. If only you and one other person are available to play, then skinny singles is a great game for you that also helps with your doubles game.

Skinny singles is played on half the court. There are many variations. The illustrations below should help – also check out the videos in the Catalog.

With every variation, the half of the court you are not playing on is out of bounds and a ball landing there ends the rally. Each side serves until a loss. Because there is no partner, there is no second server. Therefore, there are only two numbers called for the score (E.g. 3-1 instead of 3-1-1).

Option 1 – Straight Skinny Singles

You can play skinny singles straight on. You serve and play the entire game down the common sideline and do not switch left to right. The other half of the court, as indicated, is out of bounds.

For the area inside the NVZ, which does not have a line, just use your best judgment if the ball was in or out.

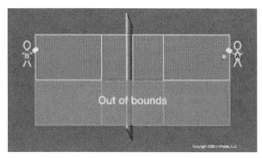

You can play on either side of the court. All the regular rules of play apply, including the Two-Bounce Rule and NVZ.

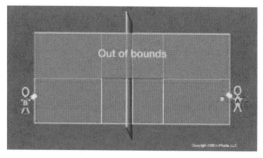

Option 2 – Cross-Court Skinny Singles

You can also play cross-court skinny singles. You serve, return, and play the rally on the right side for the whole game (never switching to the left). All other regular rules apply.

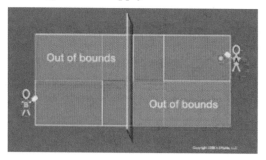

After you play a game of right side to right side, mix it up by playing left side to left side. When playing cross-court, playing the different angles will make a difference. You can play these games to 5 or 7 points.

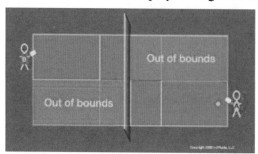

Option 3 – Full-Court Skinny Singles

To play the most complete version of skinny singles, start the game right side to right side (like a regular doubles game). This rally is played cross-court skinny singles.

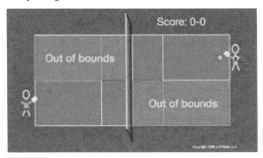

If Player A wins the first rally, Player A scores a point and moves to the left side to serve. Player B remains on the right side of the court. The serve will be straight, and the rally will be played straight, as shown.

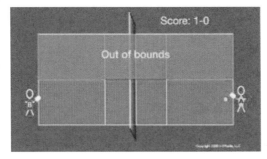

Each player's position is consistent with the player's score. Player B has zero points: right side. Player A has 1 point: left side.

VIPickleball

Player B wins the next rally. No point is scored. The serve switches from Player A to Player B. In singles play, there is only one service loss for a side out. The players stay where they were and play this rally straight.

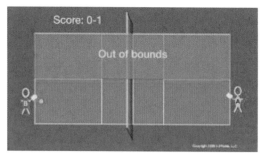

Player B wins the rally, Player B scores a point and moves to the left side to serve. Player A remains on the left side of the court. This rally is played cross-court, as shown.

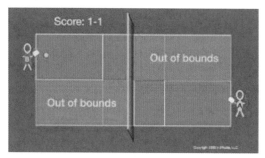

Player A wins the rally. Side out. No point is scored. Player A to serve. Score remains 1-1 and the players remain in the same positions.

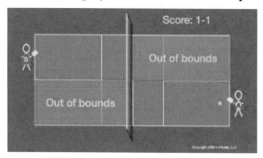

Player A wins the rally, scores a point and moves to the right side to serve again. This rally is played straight.

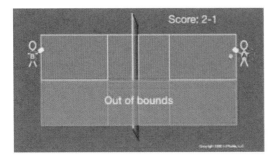

Different from regular play, the returner in skinny singles does not move to the side that is diagonal (cross-court) from the server. The returner's position is based on the returner's score.

Player B wins the rally. Side out. No point is scored. Player B to serve. Player B has 1 point – left side. Player A has 2 points – right side.

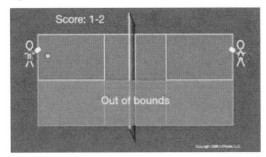

Player B wins the rally, scores a point, and moves to the right side to serve again. This rally is played cross-court, as shown.

Play continues until agreed-upon game score.

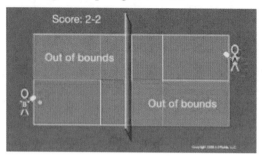

Three Players

What if there are only three of you available to play? No problem – you can still play. One side will play doubles and the other side will play singles. The singles side will normally be skinny (same as above). Or if you want more exercise, then you can play the whole court.

The singles side serves. If the singles side wins the rally, it scores a point and serves again to the other player. If the doubles side wins the rally, then all players rotate clockwise, and the new singles player serves. Players track their own score. You can play up to as many points as you want.

Except for the half-court that is out of bounds and the scoring rotation, all the regular play rules apply.

Player C starts the game on the single-player side, serves the ball, and plays skinny singles on the half of the court where Player C served. The side with the two players will play as if it were a doubles game.

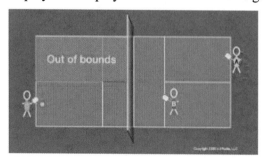

Player C wins the first rally, scores 1 point and moves to the left to serve again. Players A and B shift front to back (as they would in a doubles game), so that Player B is now the returner.

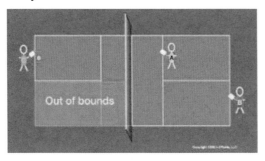

Players A and B win the next rally. No point is scored. The players rotate clockwise as shown.

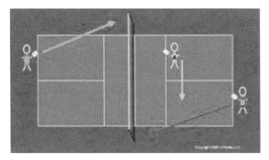

Player B will serve the next rally as shown. Players keep track of their own score (scoring points only when winning the rally on their serve). As an option, you can play a game to five points and then switch the order. For example, the players could arrange A-C-B order (clockwise) to switch things up.

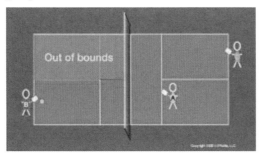

Dink Game

With four players, the dink game is a great way to work on a soft touch and purposeful placement of the ball. All four players play at the NVZ line; two people on each side. You serve and keep score as if you are playing a regular game. The rules:

1. Your serve must land inside the NVZ.
2. You can ONLY dink. Slams or hard shots are not allowed.
3. You can volley (as long as you are not inside the NVZ when you volley) but the volley must still land inside the opposite NVZ.
4. If the ball lands outside the NVZ (or sideline), point or side out.
5. When you score a point, you switch sides with your partner as in a regular game.
6. The first three dinks are cooperative to start the point and make sure everyone gets a chance to hit the ball.

Player A serves a dink shot to Player C. Player A may (highly recommended) bounce the ball to start the point. All balls must land inside the NVZ (lines are in).

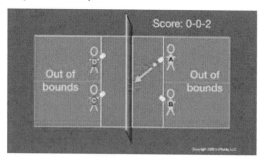

Player C dinks the ball to Player B. This is a cooperative dink – a friendlier dink to get some practice and also get the point going.

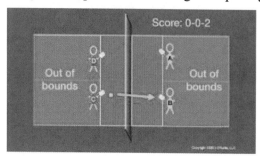

Player B will dink the ball to Player D. This is another cooperative dink. At this point, every player on the court has touched the ball.

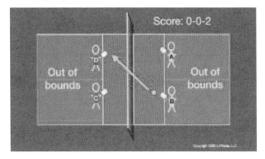

Player D may hit the next dink anywhere in the opponent's NVZ. Starting with this dink, the dinks do not have to be cooperative and instead should be aimed at applying maximum pressure on the opponents with the intent of generating a miss or a pop up.

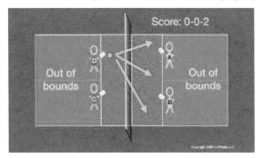

If the yellow team wins the first rally, it scores a point and Players A and B will switch left to right so that Player A is serving to Player D. The cooperative dinks will be from Player D to Player B, then from Player B to Player C. Player C's dink, and every dink after, is no longer cooperative and can be aimed anywhere (as long as it is a dink).

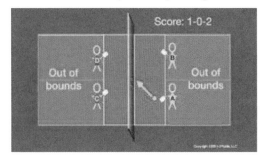

Blue team wins the next rally. Side out. No point is scored and serve switches to the blue team. Player C is server 1. Serve is Player C to Player B. Cooperative dinks are Player B to Player D, then Player D to Player A. From Player A onward everyone is trying to win the point.

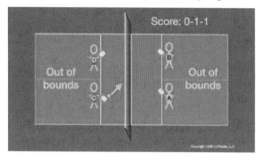

Yellow team wins the next rally. Player D is server 2. Cooperative dinks: Player A to Player C, then Player C to Player B. Player B is the first player who can come out of the cooperative dink (be aggressive).

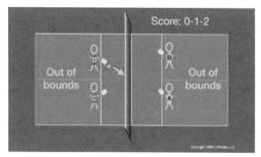

Play to as many points as agreed. An interesting variation is to play 5-point mini-games and then rotate clockwise one spot and play again. It is a chance to see different shots from different players on the court.

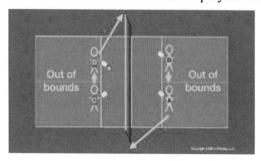

Get Out There and Play

People who try pickleball for the first time want to get out there and play ... again ... and again! Pickleball, just like every sport, has its unwritten "rules" that players just know and follow. The following include a few of these rules that you should know and that will help you feel more comfortable playing on any court across the country (or world).

In this section, we share with you:

- Some of the "unwritten rules of the road" or etiquette guidelines when playing.
- Suggested protocol when playing.

Once you get familiar with them, check out the Games section, get out there, and play.

Paddle tap

Pickleball players tap paddles with one another. It is a thing. Paddle taps are used as a way of showing support between partners on the court – think of a high five on the basketball court or soccer pitch. If your partner holds the paddle towards you, your partner is looking for you to tap paddles (gently).

Also, after a game, all players meet at the net and tap paddles. Make sure you head up to the net for the paddle tap – it is a thing.

Open play rotation

When you go to open play, ask a player on the sidelines how the player rotation works and where you place your paddle so you can be included. Some typical scenarios:

- All four players come off the court when the game is done and four new players go on a court. All four players place their paddles back into the rotation (might be separate paddle stacks for winners and non-winners to allow more rotation else you may end up playing with the same four players again).

• Two winners stay on the court and the other players come off the court and place their paddles back into the rotation.

• Two winners stay on but split so that they each play with one of the new players coming onto the court.

• You may also find places that have move up/move down arrangements where winners move "up" and non-winners move "down." This is called ladder play.

> Courts may be assigned by skill level. If you do not know your skill level yet, watch a few games. Then place your paddle to join a group of equal ability.

It is good to know how many points each game is played to at the facility. A regulation pickleball game is usually to 11 points. If courts are crowded, some facilities lower the game scores to seven or nine points. Just be aware that the game may not be to 11 points.

No matter where you go, the courts will generally have some sort of system to organize order of play (e.g., paddle stack or eraser board). Ask when you arrive to make sure you are in the rotation. It may help to notate your name on your paddle with a marker or sticker so that you can be called when it is your turn. Bottom line about open play: enjoy the social interaction and camaraderie.

Asking to play

Pickleball is a social sport; however, there are times when you may be unsure if a group is accepting walk-ons or how the play there works. Always feel free to ask pickleball players if it is an open group. Wait until the game is over or until they take a break.

If they say "no," do not be discouraged. You will find people to play. Use social media or Google to find pickleball groups in your area. Remember also that you can use Places2Play.org to find more pickleball facilities.

Out balls

There are a few things that will sour a fun pickleball game more than a questionable out call. If your opponent calls your ball out, and you disagree, it does not matter. As well as just a suggested protocol, that is the rule You accept the call and move on.

When you are making a call and you are not 100 percent sure the ball was out, just play on or give your opponent the point. Remember, a ball that lands on the line is "in." Call should not outweigh the gain of having fun on the court.

Faults

There are written rules and we have to abide by them. The same as out ball though, having some perspective when calling rules violations (or faults) will result in a more rewarding experience on the courts.

If the rules violation was minor or did not give your opponent a competitive advantage, then perhaps consider letting that one slide. Here are a couple of specific examples:

- A player's serve is technically illegal (contacted too high for example). Unless the player is using the illegal serve motion to gain an advantage by beaming balls into the court, that is one you can probably let slide. You never know. Could be a person who has shoulder pain when swinging the paddle.

- The player's foot slid forward and maybe touched the NVZ line. Is it worth stopping the game to call a fault? The decision is yours, but, trust us, nothing throws a cold bucket of water on a game faster than a minor NVZ line fault call.

The Teachers

As with anything in life, you will come across pickleball players eager to "teach" you how to play. They will share rules, "how-tos," and everything that the player thinks you should know about pickleball – many are enthusiastic about the game.

While we are not suggesting you to be rude to any of the informal local teachers of the game, we recommend you maintain a courteous but critical eye to information learned at the local courts. Some tips, like getting up to the NVZ after a return of serve, will be good advice. But there are also several "folk tales" shared on pickleball courts about the best strategy or technique.

If you are unsure about something you have heard on the courts, check it against one of the reputable online resources. There are plenty of free resources out there that you can take advantage of that will provide you with a more comprehensive understanding of the game. The following are some of our favorites (you can find much of their content on YouTube):

Pickleball – A Sport for Life

By becoming acquainted with the peculiarities of pickleball etiquette, rules of the road and open-play protocols, you can feel comfortable playing anywhere. As you become a more seasoned player, adjust your expectations about calling faults. But always remember that you, too, were once new to the sport.

As you play with more people and in different locations, you will tap paddles with some amazing players that may soon become your closest friends. Pickleball is a life-changing sport. Let it change your life.

Hope to see you some day on the courts and good luck out there!

Your Pickleball Home

Made in the USA
Middletown, DE
04 December 2021